better together*

*This book is best read together, grownup and kid.

 akidsco.com

a
kids
book
about

a kids book about BANNED books

by the National Coalition Against Censorship

a
kids
book
about

A Kids Book About books are available online: *akidsco.com*

To share your stories, ask questions, or inquire about bulk
purchases (schools, libraries, and nonprofits), please use
the following email address: *hello@akidsco.com*

ISBN: 978-1-953955-70-8

Designed by Duke Stebbins
Edited by Ashley Simpo

For every reader who has found a friend in a book.

And for the brave students, writers, teachers, and librarians who fight to make sure all kids can read books that matter to them.

Intro

Book banning is as old as book reading. Not everyone agrees on what kids should learn and when they should read books with certain themes. At the National Coalition Against Censorship, a big part of our work has been to protect free expression, which is both a basic human right and a keystone of democracy.

NCAC believes in kids' right to read. While individual parents can determine what's right for their own kids, they can't be allowed to dictate what all kids read, know, and believe.

Books raise questions, especially about unfamiliar ideas and situations. We think that's wonderful, and that questions which start conversations are always a good thing. Restricting what kids can read directly limits what they can learn, think, and talk about.

Book bans often increase when there is political and social change. During such times, we hope this book helps kids understand they can stay curious, ask questions, and speak up for what they believe in.

WAR

NING!

Some people don't want you to read this book.

 This is a book about books.

Some people think books can be

DANGEROUS,

SCARY,

or too grown up.

But we think you should get to decide for yourself.

To do that, you have to read the book (the *whole* book).

So, who are "**we**"?

We are the **National Coalition***
Against Censorship*, and we have
been defending kids' right to read
for a LONG time.

Coalition is a team working together.

*Censorship is when ideas, books, and art are changed
because someone in charge doesn't agree with them.*

Why do **you** read books?

We know people read books
for all kinds of reasons,

LIKE...

TO LEARN

new ideas, events from history, other ways of living.

TO DISCOVER

different beliefs, exciting characters*, how other people see the world.

*Characters are the people in the stories you read.

TO EXPLORE

far away places, how you see the world.

TO FEEL

*joy, sadness, excitement,
and to feel connected and seen.*

And sometimes we
read books for fun!

Not everyone likes every book.

And that's OK.

Some books have ideas that make people feel nervous or uncomfortable.

When this happens,
they may want to *ban* the book...

BANNING BOOKS

is when books are taken away from (or kept out of) a place where a lot of books can be found, like a school or library.

A book ban IS:

when a book is taken out of a library or school because someone (usually *not* a teacher or librarian) says they don't think it's right for kids.

when someone tells a librarian or teacher that they can't let kids read certain books because they personally don't believe kids should read them.

A book ban ISN'T:

when a library doesn't have space for a book.

when a book is removed because it hasn't been checked out in awhile.

when a teacher or librarian uses their professional experience to decide which books to keep.

You might be wondering,

how can a book be banned when
it can still be found on the internet
and in bookstores?

Well, every kid's access
to books is different.

For some people, schools and libraries are the only places they can find books to read, so it's very important that **one** person's opinion doesn't change what schools and libraries look like for **everyone**.

*Let's think about the books
that matter most to you...*

What books
over and

do you read over?

Think about why!

Who are the characters you love?

Have you ever read a book and thought, *that character is just like me?*

Has a book ever taught you something new about the world?

Did a story ever help you understand someone else's life?

Those helped become you

books you who are.

But what if those books were banned?

Without books that challenge you, stretch your brain, and teach you new things...

You learn less.

You discover less.

You explore less.

You feel less.

Book bans not only hurt kids who have fewer books at home or less access to books, but also:

kids who feel different from their friends.

kids who feel lonely.

kids who don't often read about characters who look like them, sound like them, love like them, or live like them.

Books are a huge way we learn about other people and develop empathy, *which means feeling **with** someone and not just **for** someone.*

The world is better when we have empathy for others.

So
book
really
EVER

bans hurt

YONE.

*If book bans hurt everyone,
why do people try to ban books?*

Lots of reasons, really...

People try to ban books because they
disagree with the ideas, characters,
or lessons inside.

But hiding things
we don't like
doesn't make
them go away.

Mostly, people try to ban books when they're afraid of what those books might help you learn, discover, explore, or feel.

And they're afraid of the questions you might ask.

We believe questions are important because questions lead to *conversations*.

And conversations are how we make **new ideas**.

We also believe it's important to learn about ideas you may disagree with.

Because you will meet A LOT of people in your life, and you won't agree with everyone you meet.

It's important to learn how to have conversations with people who think differently than you do.

As we hear new ideas, we get to shape and reshape our own opinions about the world.

We all get to be lifelong learners!

So **WHO** gets to

decide what we read?

We think no **one person**
should get to
make that choice
for **everyone**.

Everyone should make that decision for themselves.

And if you're a kid, maybe that means deciding with your grownup.

Also, teachers and librarians know a lot about how kids read and learn, so they can help guide you and answer your questions.

Not every book is right for everyone, or at least not right for them *right now*.

But all of us need access to books that help us **grow**, **learn**, and **feel seen**.

So, if someone is trying to
ban a book at your school, try this:

1 Talk to your grownup about reading the book together.

2 Read the whole book.

3 Ask questions: *Why do people dislike it? Why would someone want to ban it?*

4 Talk about what you learned and how the book made you feel.

5 If you think the book is important, take action! You could draw a picture, write a letter, or talk to your teacher or school librarian about why you think the book matters.

Books are being banned in schools and libraries every day, maybe even in a town near you.

So it's important to keep reading books, talking about them, and speaking up when someone tries to ban them.

Because the best way to fight a book ban is to call it out and say,

"I DON'T AGREE WITH THIS."

Remember, you (and your grownup) know what's right for you.

And everyone deserves to choose
what's right for them.

Outro

Now that you and your kid have talked about banned books and how they impact our world, you may be wondering what else you can do. Both kids and grownups can advocate for their right to have access to a wide range of reading choices. Not every book is right for every kid, or right for every kid right now. And that really is OK. Parents and caregivers can ask for other school readings and limit what their kids are able to check out from the library. But no one person should get to decide what all kids can read based on their own personal opinions and beliefs.

NCAC offers a variety of free resources for anyone who wants to advocate for books in their communities. We also offer guidance and advice for censorship disputes. Resources and a censorship reporting tool are on our website NCAC.org.